# A Biblical Worldview on Racism

© Copyright 2024 – Andrew Wommack

Printed in the United States of America. All rights reserved. No portion of this book may be reproduced, stored in a retrieval system, or transmitted in any form or by any means—electronic, mechanical, photocopy, recording, scanning, or other—except for brief quotations in critical reviews or articles, without the prior written permission of the publisher.

Unless otherwise indicated, all Scripture quotations are taken from the King James Version® of the Bible. Copyright © by the British Crown. Public domain.

Scripture quotations marked NKJV are taken from the New King James Version®. Copyright © 1982 by Thomas Nelson. Used by permission. All rights reserved.

"Scripture quotations taken from the (NASB®) New American Standard Bible®, Copyright © 1960, 1971, 1977, 1995 by The Lockman Foundation. Used by permission. All rights reserved. lockman.org"

"Scripture quotations are from The ESV® Bible (The Holy Bible, English Standard Version®), © 2001 by Crossway, a publishing ministry of Good News Publishers. Used by permission. All rights reserved."

All emphasis within Scripture quotations is the author's own.

Published in partnership between Andrew Wommack Ministries and Harrison House Publishers.

Woodland Park, CO 80863 – Shippensburg, PA 17257

ISBN 13 TP: 978-1-59548-644-8

For Worldwide Distribution, Printed in the USA

1 2 3 4 5 6 / 27 26 25 24

# CONTENTS

Introduction .................................................................. 1

**Chapter 1** Racism Revealed
by E.W. Jackson ....................................................... 3

**Chapter 2** A Biblical Refutation of Racism
by Andrew Wommack ............................................ 9

**Chapter 3** Historical Facts about Racism
by Abraham Hamilton III ...................................... 15

**Chapter 4** The Gospel: The Solution to Ethnic Tension
by Abraham Hamilton III ...................................... 21

**Chapter 5** Victories over Racism
by David Barton and Tim Barton ............ 27

**Chapter 6** Civil Rights Used Wrongly
by Alex McFarland ......................................... 33

**Chapter 7** Racism and the Danger of Losing America
by E.W. Jackson .................................................... 39

**Chapter 8** Exposing Progressivism's Role in
Encouraging Racism Today
by David Barton and Tim Barton ............ 45

**Chapter 9** Truth in a World of "Hate Speech"
by Alex McFarland .................................................. 51

**Chapter 10** God's Church as the Standard Bearer
by Andrew Wommack .................................................. 57

Conclusion .................................................................. 63

Continue Building Your Biblical Worldview ............ 65

Receive Jesus as Your Savior .................................... 67

Receive the Holy Spirit ............................................. 69

*Note: This booklet is just a brief introduction to twelve hours of teaching from the* Biblical Worldview: Racism *curriculum. Statistics included in the **"Did You Know?"** and text sections of this booklet were cited when the complete curriculum was originally published and may no longer represent the most current information.*

*About a Biblical Worldview*

Everyone views the world based on their beliefs—it's their worldview. As you process everything that you encounter, whether you know it or not, you are looking at it through a lens based on a variety of influences. You filter life based on experiences and factors from your background, such as where you grew up, family dynamics, ethnic heritage, religious upbringing, education and educators' views shared with students, and political views. Every day, your worldview guides your thoughts, decisions, and conversations.

It may surprise you to know that Christians don't automatically have a biblical worldview. When you became a Christian, you just began a journey to renew your mind. You did not automatically get a biblical worldview download at salvation. The problem many Christians face is a clash of worldviews. Often, it is difficult to recognize the daily assault on their Christian values and biblical teachings. Take note the next time you hear a news report or people sharing their perspectives and if you feel a twinge inside that indicates something isn't sitting right in your spirit. Typically, people are busy and ignore that twinge. When someone regularly encounters and hears perspectives that conflict with God's truth, that person can become dulled to it and simply begin to accept those perspectives as truth.

# INTRODUCTION

These days, people often use the word "racism" as a trigger to promote hatred. Sadly, most people choose to believe the media and education system's new revisions to American History. An honest look at the history of racism doesn't only look at the issue of slavery in America starting in 1619. To understand the topic, we must look to the Bible to discover the true beginnings of racism and slavery. The book of Genesis reveals several truths about racism. This booklet will help you uncover facts about how many races God says exist and the root cause of racism.

Is there a right or wrong attitude toward racism and prejudice? What should Christians say or do? Throughout this booklet, you will discover that God has much to say about the importance of knowing the truth because the truth sets people free (John 8:32). By building an arsenal of biblical principles, you will be empowered to shine light into a dark world as you speak truth about the divisive topic of racism.

This booklet guides you to discern between what the Bible says and today's popular narrative about racism. A biblical worldview provides Christians with a unique roadmap to discover the truth about racism that helps heal those wounded by the lies. As you unravel the lies of racism, you discover the simple truth— racism is not a skin problem but a sin problem!

# CHAPTER 1

# RACISM REVEALED

by E.W. Jackson

America has discussed race for 400 years, but the issue remains. Racial conflict and animosity continue to plague us because we don't understand the issue properly. The solution to racism begins with reframing the problem. For example, when a person is diagnosed with cancerous tumors, the doctor removes the tumors. But will that ultimately cure the person from cancer? No, because the underlying problem is the cancer. The tumors are just a symptom, and they will keep growing. Similarly, people today approach race like that doctor. They cut away the tumors without treating the underlying cause. The underlying cause of racism has nothing to do with race, but it has to do with a deeper human problem—sin.

The United States is not a racist country, but like any other country, it is plagued by sin. Although laws get passed and civil rights breakthroughs happen, the United States still deals with racism. We must acknowledge that **racism is not a skin problem but a sin problem**. Sin created a division between God and Adam, and it ultimately caused Cain to kill Abel. The relationship between sin and division is repeated throughout the Bible.

The Egyptians, who enslaved the children of Israel, weren't Europeans or White. God delivered the Israelites out of that slavery and bondage. The twelve tribes of Israel were of the same lineage, yet they couldn't get along. The tribes of Judah and Benjamin divided against the other ten tribes, who became the northern kingdom. These two kingdoms fought throughout history until both kingdoms fell. This was tribalism, which is another "tumor" with the same underlying "disease" of sin. The northern kingdom collapsed in 721 BC, and they became the Samaritans.[1] The New Testament records Jesus dealing with racism when He met a Samaritan woman at the well who described the division between her people and the Jews, saying, *"How is it that You, being a Jew, ask a drink from me, a Samaritan woman? For Jews have no dealings with Samaritans"* (John 4:9 NKJV).

Division is common, but unlike other nations, America was founded on biblical principles that speak to our consciences and do not allow us to treat people as less than humans. These principles caused Christians to grapple with sin and God's command to love one another. As a result, many Christians stood against slavery and racism then and now. If the country has always been racist, why was there opposition to segregation? Not only did Black people oppose segregation, but Americans of all backgrounds did.

> **Did You Know?**
>
> History reveals the problem is not about skin color. Anthony Johnson was a Black indentured servant in colonial America. He became a landowner after gaining his freedom around 1635. He saw the enslavement of Black people, yet he fought to have slaves. In 1830 in the South, there were approximately 169,000 free Blacks and over 3,700 Black slave owners who owned 12,000 slaves. It's not a story that you hear much because it doesn't quite fit the narrative.[2]

The question that Christians must ask is, how can I hate you or look down on you because you have a different complexion than I do? God made you. You didn't choose how you look. You didn't choose your ancestral background—God did. Racism is the equivalent of telling God, "You didn't know what You were doing. You were wrong to create that. I would do better. I would create people who look like me." That arrogant attitude has no place in our hearts, homes, or churches.

America is an imperfect country. It is not heaven, but there is no country on earth that looks more like what the kingdom of God looks like than the United States of America. Revelation 7:9 (NKJV) says this about heaven,

> *"...and behold, a great multitude which no one could number, of all nations, tribes, peoples, and tongues, standing before the throne and before the Lamb..."*

Only one nation on the earth has people from every part of the globe. In heaven, you won't stand with your ethnic group. You will stand before God on your own and only give an account for your deeds. You will not make excuses about what your background was and what somebody else told you to think. Let's start looking at each other as individuals because that's the way it will be in heaven, and that's the way God will judge us.

# CHAPTER 2
# A BIBLICAL REFUTATION OF RACISM
## by Andrew Wommack

No biblical reasons exist to reject a person because of skin color or ethnicity. Under the Old Testament law, if you cursed your parents, you could be put to death (Lev. 20:9). It was *"an eye for an eye, and a tooth for a tooth"* (Matt. 5:38). With the Old Covenant, once people gave themselves over to demonic activity, the only way to purge that was to destroy those people. That's the reason the Lord told His people not to associate or intermarry with other people groups. God wasn't prejudiced or believed certain nations were better than others. God wanted His people to avoid others who had given themselves over to Satan. The Lord was protecting His people.

Jesus clearly stated that things were different under the New Covenant. God didn't change, but people changed because they can be born again. With the New Covenant, people were no longer killed who committed sodomy or adultery because they could be born again and redeemed.

Throughout the Bible we find guidance on the issue of racism. John 3:16 says, *"For God so loved the world."* He didn't love only a certain ethnic group. He loved the whole world. Couple that verse with Romans 10:13: *"For whosoever shall call upon the name of the Lord shall be saved."* If Jesus died for and accepts everybody, what right do we have to reject anyone?

People are made in the image of God (Gen. 1:26), and we need to love people. Color or physical differences between ethnic groups don't matter. Every person alive on this planet came through Adam and Eve.

Acts 17:26 says that God has made every nation from "one blood." The blood is where our life comes from. *"For the life of the flesh is in the blood..."* (Lev. 17:11). Pigment of the skin is a minor difference among people. Physical features are not meant to be divisive or to separate us into different groups.

> **Did You Know?**
>
> It is a sin to compare and make others inferior. *"For we dare not make ourselves of the number, or compare ourselves with some that commend themselves: but they measuring themselves by themselves, and comparing themselves among themselves, are not wise"* (2 Cor. 10:12). The fallen human trait of making comparisons finds a way to make ourselves look better than others. Comparison leads to racism.

Some people look for scriptures to empower what they already believe. Even the Jews fell into deception and thought they were God's only chosen people. Jesus responded and said, *"God is able of these stones to raise up children unto Abraham"* (Matt. 3:9). The Jews misinterpreted Scripture like some people today who believe God chose only one ethnic group and rejected all others.

Galatians 3:28 says, *"There is neither Jew nor Greek, there is neither bond nor free, there is neither male nor female: for ye are all one in Christ Jesus."* This verse does not say there aren't Jews, Greeks, or slaves. However, believers shouldn't relate to other people based on whether we are male or female, bond or free, or Jew or gentile. We are all one in Christ.

Because of sin, the Lord sent the flood (Gen. 6). Later, Noah's descendants built the Tower of Babel because their hearts became evil, and they unified against God. So, God separated them into different languages and nations. There is a place for nations, boundaries between nations, family units, and community units. But to reject one group over another is contrary to what Scripture says.

If you say you love God and hate other people, you're a liar. If you believe the Bible, then it leaves no place for racism or rejecting a person over any physical trait. If you were taught prejudice, it may take a while to renew your mind. If you humble yourself, the Lord will show you there is no reason to exalt yourself over anybody else or put anybody else down. We are all children of God, and we should love each other.

## CHAPTER 3

# HISTORICAL FACTS ABOUT RACISM

by Abraham Hamilton III

Scripture and church history give evidence that Christianity thrived in Africa throughout history. This dispels the argument suggesting that Christianity is the White man's religion. The people who gathered in Jerusalem to celebrate the Passover Feast, were "from every nation" (Acts 2:5). Those 3,120 Pentecost converts came from modern-day Iran, Iraq, Kuwait, Egypt, Israel, Jordan, Turkey, Greece, Libya, Tunisia, and Algeria. Besides geographic and ethnic diversity, they were also diverse linguistically (Acts 2:8–11).

Soon after Pentecost, persecution against Christians broke out, and believers spread around the world. They went to Phoenicia, to the Greek island of Cyprus, and to Antioch, which is in modern-day Syria (Acts 11:19–30). The first believers to evangelize Antioch were from the Greek island of Cyprus and from the African country of Cyrene, or modern-day Libya (Acts 11:20). To clarify, some of the first people to preach the Gospel in the first century were African Christians.

In Antioch, followers of Jesus Christ *"were called Christians first in Antioch"* (Acts 11:26). The term Christian was a derisive insult. The culture in Antioch was such that they couldn't believe this diverse mix of people came together in unity. They sounded like Jesus. They acted like Jesus. They treated each other the way that Jesus encouraged them to treat each other. They also called them levelers. Within the family of God, someone on the bottom rung in Antiochian culture could be an elder in the church. The outsiders called them levelers because in Christ, *"There is neither Jew nor Greek, there is neither slave nor free"* (Gal. 3:28 NKJV). At the foot of the cross, we are all equal in our need of salvation.

The Gentile church in Antioch could be considered the first mega-church and included African eldership (Acts 13:1–3). It mentions a man by the name of Simeon, who was called Niger. At that time, Antioch was under Roman control, and the dominant Roman language was Latin. The word *Niger* is Latin for "black." They described Simeon by his skin color. Then, Scripture mentions Lucius of Cyrene. Simeon and Lucius were both from African nations. They laid hands on Paul and Barnabas and commissioned them to their Gospel work.

In the second century, Tertullian helped shape Christianity. He was an African theologian and apologist from Carthage, Tunisia. At that time, philosophers debated everything. Tertullian argued there was no need for pagan philosophers to navigate, interpret, and apply Scripture. The Word of God is enough. Tertullian was the first person to use the term Trinity to describe the Godhead—one substance, three persons.[3]

In the mid-fourth to fifth century, Augustine was another influential African church scholar and theologian. He was born in the modern-day nation of Algeria. He was credited for almost single-handedly shaping the entire Western Christian tradition throughout the Middle Ages.[4] His book, *Confessions*, details his life and conversion to Christianity. This book was the first autobiography written in Western literature.[5] It is not a stretch to say that Africa helped shape the Christian mind. One fact obscured from history is that these men all were African.

> **Did You Know?**
> Ethiopian Christianity began in the first century and helped shape the Protestant Reformation. In his writings, Martin Luther mentioned Ethiopia at least eighty-five times.[6] Acts 8 profiles the Ethiopian credited with converting the Ethiopian kingdom to Christ. Ethiopia was the first Christian kingdom in history.[6] For Luther, the Ethiopian church became the forerunner of Protestantism.

The Bible and church history show that all people descend from one common ancestry. God revealed to Abram that *"in you all the families of the earth shall be blessed"* (Gen. 12:3 NKJV). On the Day of Pentecost, people came from many nations. The church received the Holy Spirit, and the Gospel was proclaimed in power. The book of Revelation culminates when people from all nations, tribes, and tongues gather around God's throne (Rev. 7:9–11). May the body of Christ realize it is equipped to navigate the issues of our day by standing firmly on the truth of God's Word.

CHAPTER 4

# THE GOSPEL: THE SOLUTION TO ETHNIC TENSION

by Abraham Hamilton III

In many conversations about justice and equality, Christians listen to what the world says rather than standing on what the Word of God says. The Word of God tells us that *"From one man he created all the nations throughout the whole earth"* (Acts 17:26 NLT). The word nation from the Scripture is ethnos in Greek,[7] where we get the English word "ethnicity." According to Scripture, there is no such thing as many races of human beings. There are various people groups and ethnicities. On March 12, 2018, *National Geographic* published an article, "There's No Scientific Basis for Race—It's a Made-up Label."[8] Amazingly, the scientific community is catching up to the biblical truth that there is no such thing as many races of human beings.

> **Did You Know?**
>
> The concept we know as *races* stems from the mid-nineteenth century work of Samuel Morton. He objected to the biblical notion of creation, which he described as "monogenism." He said various skin colors of people indicated there were many creation events called "polygenism."[9] He opined that there were many races of people, and that skin color was indicative of where we were as a society in the evolutionary developmental process.[9] Morton's work was then built upon by Charles Darwin.

There is one race called the human race. As Christ's followers, we should stand firmly on the Word of God to communicate this fact to others. Jesus says, *"Blessed are the peacemakers, for they shall be called sons of God"*

(Matt. 5:9 NASB95). Peacemakers are distinct from peacekeepers. Peacekeepers maintain peace inherited from elsewhere. Peacemakers forge peace out of chaos. It is important that we commit ourselves to being peacemakers rather than peacekeepers.

The Bible demonstrates the mechanism to address ethnic tension in our modern context through the early church as shown in the book of Acts. The first-century church, mentioned in Acts 2–4, exploded in growth in the face of socioeconomic, political, and ethnic tensions. People with different languages and from different cultures spent time together in the instruction of Scripture, the teaching of the apostle, prayer, and fellowship. The group practiced koinonia[10], which means fellowship, and breaking bread together. Acts 11:27–30 says the Gentile church in Antioch—many of whom were treated disparately by Jewish leaders—learned of a famine in Jerusalem.

They put their funds and resources together and sent money because the Gospel is the way.

According to the Word of God, the body of Christ is positioned to navigate racial issues. Proverbs 28:5 says, *"Evil men do not understand justice, but those who seek the Lord understand it completely"* (ESV). In conversations about justice, evil men are incapable of navigating the issue appropriately, but the Christ follower understands it completely. This scripture encourages us to refuse to retreat. We should enter these conversations with confidence. When wicked men drive the dialogue concerning justice, they seek conciliation void of the cross. The conversation descends from a pursuit of justice into a pursuit of vengeance. In our modern society, there are efforts to pursue reconciliation, but they omit the cross.

Reconciliation happens through Jesus. It is our job to maintain unity. It is not our job to create reconciliation. In fact, it's the opposite (Eph. 2:16). We first become reconciled to God. As a result of reconciliation to God by the blood of Jesus Christ, we become reconciled to one another. Later, Paul instructs us to give all diligence *"to preserve the unity of the Spirit in the bond of peace"* (Eph. 4:3, NASB95). It is our job to preserve what God has secured for us. We have unity through praying together, breaking bread together, and fellowshipping. As we grow in our relationships in the body of Christ, we learn about one another, learn what others' needs are, and meet each other's needs.

Understanding the love ethic found in Scripture and combining it with intimate fellowship shows us how the Gospel works. In the first century, the Romans, Arabs, Algerians,

Tunisians, and Jews found unity by submitting to the teaching of Scripture, praying together, and breaking bread together. The result was unity, and the church grew in the first century. The same unity is available today if we follow what Christ has called us to obey. We can re-submit ourselves to the teaching of Scripture and understand that the Gospel soothes ethnic tensions.

## CHAPTER 5

# VICTORIES OVER RACISM
## by David Barton and Tim Barton

American history is not purely a White history. Today's retelling of history excludes many important non-White people from American history. Now the narrative focuses on racism and discrimination. That did exist because Americans were humans, and humans sin. However, if you focus only on racism, you miss all the other stories of racial victory.

George Washington's army was a volunteer army. Black patriots on average voluntarily served significantly longer than White patriots did. White patriots would average about six months enlisted. Black patriots averaged four-and-a-half years in the military.[11] It's also significant that Blacks and Whites fought side by side. They didn't have many segregated units. Blacks and Whites fought together in virtually every battle in the American War for Independence.[12]

There are many notable Black patriots from the American Revolution. The famous painting of the Battle of Bunker Hill by John Trumbull contains Peter Salem, a Black patriot known as the hero of the Battle of Bunker Hill.[13] Salem shot the British officer leading the charge, Major Pitcairn.[14] This stopped the British charge. The Americans gained time to escape British capture and death. More than a dozen American officers wanted him honored because he saved their lives.

Another example of Black heroism occurred during the last major battle of the American Revolution, the Battle of Yorktown. Washington tasked General Lafayette with tracking the British force's movements, especially Lord Cornwallis. Lafayette recognized that Black patriots could enter British forts pretending to be escaped slaves seeking refuge from the Revolutionaries. While they were in the British camp, they could listen to the conversations and report back to Lafayette.

A slave from Virginia named James Armistead wound up being a spy in Cornwallis' camp. Soon, Lord Cornwallis recruited James to be a spy for the British. James became the first double spy in American history. While he pretended to spy for Lord Cornwallis and the British, he spied for the Americans. James Armistead found out that Lord Cornwallis was moving with his troops to Yorktown and got that information to Lafayette.[15] Lafayette got that information to Washington, who was able to surround Yorktown by land and sea. Cornwallis surrendered, and the patriots won the Battle of Yorktown.[16] The victory at Yorktown can be credited to the intelligence given to them by this Black patriot, James Armistead.

Many people do not understand the true history of slavery and misjudge America. Here are key facts that need to be understood.

Fact #1: Slavery was inhumane and barbaric.

Fact #2: America was not a world leader in the global slave trade.

Fact #3: Recent "historical" concepts about 1619 are not accurate.

Fact #4: Free Blacks were also slave owners in America.

Fact #5: It wasn't just free Blacks or Whites who owned slaves in America.

Fact #6: There were White slaves in America.[17]

Fact #7: Muslim slave traders were responsible for much of the slavery that existed.

Fact #8: Most southern Whites never actually owned slaves.

> **Did You Know?**
>
> If you look at pictures through the late 1800s of Native American groups, you often see a Black face among the Native Americans. At the time of the 1860 census, among all the major Indian tribes, approximately 12 percent of the population were Black slaves.[18] America banned slavery in 1865. Under the Constitution, Indian tribes are considered foreign nations with separate treaties. Slavery didn't end in 1865 in the Native American tribes. The federal government renegotiated treaties with the tribes to end slavery.[19]

America is not a perfect nation. America made mistakes throughout history. It's worth asking the question, "Why did those things stop in America?" The answer always is that Christians stood up. They said, "We can't let this happen anymore." Our nation can advance in race relations by Christians getting involved. We need to consider what Dr. Martin Luther King, Jr. talked about in his "I Have a Dream Speech" and say, "We're not going to judge someone by the color of their skin, but rather by the content of their character."[20]

The Bible teaches that God separated people based on what someone did or did not do—not based on the color of their skin. America does have an impressive record when it comes to race history because Christians stood up to make a difference. Now, more than ever, our nation needs Christians to stand up again and do the same.

## CHAPTER 6

# CIVIL RIGHTS USED WRONGLY
### by Alex McFarland

Christians believe that God made people in His image. All humans have worth, value, dignity, and deserve respect—not preferential, special treatment. We have God-given natural rights so we don't need to manufacture artificial rights. All are created equal with inalienable rights. We are humans made in God's image and we believe in civil rights for all.

There is no place for hate in the life of the Christian. We are to love as Christ loved *"because he laid down his life for us"* (1 John 3:16). The Bible says that we are to love our neighbors (Matt. 22:39). We are even instructed to love our enemies (Matt. 5:44). The Bible says,

*"Greater love hath no man than this, than to lay down one's life for his friends"* (John 15:13 NKJV).

America's founding documents say that God created all people equal and gave them the right to freedom, liberty, self-determination, and to plot their own destiny.[21] In spite of this good foundation, people owned slaves. How could it be that America was a free nation, with its independence declared from Britain, and yet slaves were owned? Here in the twenty-first century, people are trying to use unjust acts to remedy long-past injustices. Slavery was wrong in all forms. It was wrong of Africans to enslave their countrymen and sell them to Islamic and European traders. It was wrong for Blacks or Whites to buy trafficked Africans.[22] It was wrong for colonists to buy them and use them to clear lands, grow crops, and build plantations. Categorically, emphatically, and unequivocally, slavery was wrong.

In the twenty-first century, do we atone for slavery by committing present injustices? Do we tell all Caucasians they are systemically and structurally racist? Does demonizing one ethnicity now atone for an injustice from two hundred years ago? It really doesn't. Our nation finds itself in the dangerous position of moving beyond civil rights to special rights.

The right course of action is rarely a mystery. The United States based its civil government on biblical principles, and yet slavery existed. Many of the Founders were born-again believers and knew slavery was wrong. Thomas Jefferson prohibited the "importation of slaves into any port or place within the jurisdiction of the United States." The Constitution was written in 1787. Within twenty years, President Jefferson proclaimed America would no longer import slaves.[23]

The Civil War and the signature of the Emancipation Proclamation by Republican President Abraham Lincoln ended slavery.[24] Even after the Civil Rights Bill of 1866 was legislated,[25] it was the Democrat-led South that created the Jim Crow laws that were heinously perpetuated to shame Black Americans and to withhold basic human needs. Blacks couldn't eat in restaurants or stay in the same hotels with Whites.[26]

Only one nation fought an internal civil war with itself to end slavery: the United States. America was based on Judeo-Christian values. The Founders knew that slavery and our free nation were incompatible.[27] In North Carolina, the Quakers had a church called Cane Creek. They took children from the rural farms to the church house to teach them to read.[28] Why teach children to read? Why has literacy been a core value for the church for two thousand years? Because if people can read, they can read the Bible—the Word of God. The first North Carolina schools were churches.[29] The Christians built schools and universities and taught people of all strata to read.[30] Christians founded the Ivy League schools.[31] The emancipation of slaves, the elimination of slavery, and the making of our nation into a racially-just country emanated from the church.[32]

To allow slavery, many Americans abandoned their belief in natural rights, morals, and the God from whom morality emanates. It's not that America was based on the wrong philosophy or the wrong core convictions. We momentarily, in the founding of the nation, didn't honor and live by those convictions.

Now, one of the best things that we can do is to love our neighbor. We first love God, then we love those around us. We don't see skin color. We see people—people made in the image of God (Gen. 1:26), people whom God loves, and in obedience to His Word, we love them too (John 13:34).

# CHAPTER 7

# RACISM AND THE DANGER OF LOSING AMERICA

by E.W. Jackson

We must understand the nature of the racism problem before we can fix it. Americans are not educated properly and are not given correct information. We have been lied to by colleges and universities, the media, and the institutions of cultural influence. Even the corporate world places employees into indoctrination sessions to convince them that skin color determines character and requires them to repent for something that they have nothing to do with.[33]

There is a political agenda to destroy America. Some people think that free enterprise is wrong and the belief that our fundamental rights come from our Creator is wrong. They want to install a socialist utopia. They understand that before Americans will throw off the wonderful system that produced the most successful nation in the history of mankind, a sense of unrest must be created. The narrative we're told makes us think other nations are not that bad, but America is bad. They use race to stir people up, get people angry, keep people divided, and make people

> **Did You Know?**
>
> Marxism, the social and economic doctrine developed by Karl Marx and Friedrich Engels in the nineteenth century, sought to overturn culture by starting a violent revolution. The goal of Marxism was to take control of society—closing churches and businesses—and redistribute wealth to the proletariat, the lower wage-earning class.[34]

embittered. It provides an excellent emotional trigger.

Antonio Gramsci, an Italian communist, thought it wasn't necessary to close the churches. Rather, he believed that churches should change their mission so they would no longer exist for personal salvation and to help the individual follow Jesus, but instead the church's mission should be to support social justice.[35]

The subversion of Judeo-Christian values and principles began decades ago without people realizing it. The subversion of the Black family started when welfare policies incentivized men to be out of the home and women to be single-parent heads of households. They sought to destroy and break down the family. If you want people dependent upon the state, destroy the family and stop them from living independently.

Black Lives Matter, a political organization that focuses on race, subverts the culture. Founded by people who support Marxism,[36] they substitute traditional values of honor and valuing all life for values that promote class warfare and racial conflict. If Black Lives Matter cared about Black lives, they would care about the thousands of young men, women, and children who die in the streets of inner cities across this country every year at the hands of Black criminals.[37] Instead, they say absolutely nothing about it.

Organizations such as Black Lives Matter, Antifa, colleges and universities, and many of our public schools use their influence to move us toward a Marxist society. It's sad, but we must be aware of it. The communist school of thought says that there is no truth other than what the party says. It undermines the idea of absolute truth as if to say, "There's no absolute truth.[38] There's your truth and my truth." The

American Founding Fathers said, "We hold these truths to be self-evident."[39] Their truth was not opinions, not vacillating ideas to argue about. In John 14:6 Jesus said, *"...I am the way, the truth, and the life."* Not—I am *a* truth. I am *the* Truth.

We are not dealing with an economic or political problem but with a spiritual problem. We're dealing with a heart problem—a soul problem. Some people hope to create an insurmountable legacy of America as a hopelessly racist nation wrapped in social injustice. They promote capitalism and free enterprise as spreading racism, social injustice, and the unfair distribution of wealth.

Don't despair. Here are ten things we can do to save our country:

1. We need to restore individualism as the fundamental principle of our nation.

2. Ignore skin color.
3. We need to deal with others on the basis of their character.
4. We must care about one another as Americans and seek goodwill with each other rather than allowing anybody to make us enemies.
5. We've got to oppose efforts to use the past as a political weapon.
6. Keep your children out of public schools and secular universities and colleges.
7. Solve the problem of inner-city poverty.
8. Celebrate American History Month to restore respect for the nobility of American history.
9. Reinvigorate the vision proclaimed in our Pledge of Allegiance.
10. Restore faith in God as the central value of our nation.

# CHAPTER 8

# EXPOSING PROGRESSIVISM'S ROLE IN ENCOURAGING RACISM TODAY

by David Barton and Tim Barton

Two differing ideologies examine the problem of race relations and how to solve it. From a biblical perspective, it is important to know that God always looks at the individual. We do not label an entire group based on the actions or behavior of a few individuals. In the political arena, a recognizable philosophy emphasizes groups and builds policy around them. Liberals, progressives, or secularists promote this philosophy of identity politics.[40] They create their politics based on identity, not as an individual but as a group.

Putting people in groups by identity divides them and doesn't view people as God sees them. God said not to focus on what you see on the outside because you are missing the significance of who that person is on the inside (1 Sam. 16:7). God sees things differently than we do. Labeling people and putting them in groups is not God's idea. God sees humanity as the saved or the unsaved.

Progressive ideology claims that some people are different or better, more injured or persecuted, and oppressors and victims.[41] Everybody has a category. The progressive false narrative creates tension and then offers a solution to fix the problem it created. Many progressive groups promote racism. They categorize the Founding Fathers as White guys who were racist oppressors. The Black people in Early America became the victims. That does a great disservice and discredits so many amazing Black heroes from the era of the Founding Fathers.

One example of progressive ideology encouraging racism was Woodrow Wilson, who professed to be a Christian. His actions were contrary to the Word of God in many situations.[42] He became the president of Princeton and then the president of the United States of America.[43] Woodrow Wilson was a racist. He wrote the first chronological history book to tell America's story. In *A History of the American People*, he cut out every Black hero in American history. Woodrow Wilson's history books influenced the standards used in public schools beginning in the early 1900s. By copying those standards, they cut out the history of anyone who was not White.[44] After a few generations of this tainted history, we don't know our own history. That's a real problem because we don't know whether what's being said today is true or not.

> **Did You Know?**
>
> President Teddy Roosevelt welcomed immigrants, but he knew there had to be unity in a nation. He said, "There is no room in this country for hyphenated Americanism. When I refer to hyphenated Americans, I do not refer to naturalized Americans…a hyphenated American is not an American at all…The one absolutely certain way of bringing this nation to ruin would be to permit it to become a tangle of squabbling nationalities, an intricate knot of German-Americans, Irish-Americans, English-Americans, French-Americans, Scandinavian-Americans, Italian-Americans, each preserving its separate nationality. Each at heart feeling more sympathy with the Europeans of that nationality than with the other citizens of the American Republic."[45]

Another divisive tool is the 1619 Project, a major initiative from the *New York Times* observing the 400th anniversary of the beginning of American slavery. The 1619 Project talks about Jamestown as though it is the only colony that ever existed in America. That's not true. The Pilgrims of Plymouth Colony, founded the very next year, were abolitionists. When slave ships arrived, the Pilgrims freed the slaves and imprisoned the slave owners.[46] The 1619 Project aims to reframe 1619 as our true founding. It places the consequences of slavery at the center of the story we tell ourselves about who we are,[47] but our standards must be based on historical truth, not fiction.

Christians know the truth that sets us free (John 8:32). We do not want to be destroyed for a lack of knowledge (Hos. 4:6). The Bible's answer is that Jesus didn't come to save a particular group of people. Salvation is for the individual. We see this progressivism push to be in groups as a very demonic attack. It is not a God-centered idea or biblical idea.

We do not want to buy into the progressive ideology that says we need to tear down America and do something totally different. Christians need to get involved and fix the problems in America. We need to be the solution. We need to be the salt and light (Matt. 5:13-14). We need to be wise enough not to buy into false ideologies because God is more concerned with us as individuals than as a group.

## CHAPTER 9

# TRUTH IN A WORLD OF "HATE SPEECH"

by Alex McFarland

Truth is absolute. But, if we say, "Right is right, wrong is wrong, sex outside of marriage is a sin according to the Word of God, immorality is wrong, abortion is wrong," some people call that "hate speech." When we say homosexuality is wrong, the world calls us homophobic. In the quest to get away from moral truth, a whole new lexicon has been invented.

Christians say, "Truth is truth. There is morality. Right is right, and wrong is wrong." But, the Left says, "That's your truth. That's not my truth." We are being held hostage by relativism which says, "You have your truth, but I have my truth—end of story."[48] However, the law of non-contradiction refutes relativism and says, "We might all be wrong, but we can't all be right because truth is reality. If something is true, something else must be false."[49] So, the law of non-contradiction is the universal solvent that dissolves this impasse between Christians and the Left. We do not invent truth. We find truth, and we either act on it or reject it, but we reject truth at our own peril.

What do you do with two mutually exclusive, incompatible statements or contradictory propositions that cannot be reconciled? Fortunately, God wove logic into the fabric of reality. Aristotle was called the father of logic.[50] He codified many of the principles of logic: if this is true, that is false; either A or B, but not both A and B. He didn't invent logic, but he discovered it. If you're going to argue against reasoning, you have to reason in any attempt to deny rationality. Logic tells us that things are either true or false. The law of non-contradiction follows this line of reasoning. We can't have things that are both true and false. If someone is a male, by logical necessity, he is not a female.

Equality is often used as a platform to generate racial hate speech toward anyone with an opposing view. Socialism and liberalism say that the government's job is to provide everything. Christianity and American

> **Did You Know?**
> The philosophy of egalitarianism is from the Latin word *aequalitatem*, meaning "equality."[51] Egalitarianism says things should be the same or equal. We are living in a time of radical, enforced egalitarianism. Many people try to defend egalitarianism, but it paves the way for socialism.

capitalism say that everybody can have equal opportunity. We are not always going to have equal outcomes, but we will have an equal opportunity. Struggles purify our character and make us better. To go to college, you might have to work, struggle, and engage in deferred gratification. College isn't given to you. When you have to work, that's not racism. That's reality. In the world, there are inequities and situations that are unfair. But it purges us, humbles us, and causes us to turn to God.

Often, hate speech focuses on what people do not want to recognize as a sin. The Bible says sin is wrong, and there is no expiration date on sin. No religious leader, professor, or celebrity has the power to declassify any sin. Sin is still sin. It doesn't mean we are hateful, racist, biased, or phobic. It means we are being true to the Word of God. The most loving thing we can do is to tell our neighbor the truth. In fact, the most hateful thing—even worse than selfishness, greed, or racism—is to see your neighbor lost on their way to eternity without Christ. How unloving to know the way people can go to heaven and to withhold that information.

We must get back to the truth. Truth must come through pastors preaching, Christians influencing, parents raising their kids, and educators courageously speaking what is truth.

# CHAPTER 10

# GOD'S CHURCH AS THE STANDARD BEARER

by Andrew Wommack

Satan has deceived people for a very long time about racism. Today, people take race issues and try to make others feel abused and hurt. Our world isn't perfect. Certainly, there are racists and people who abuse other people. Terrible atrocities have been perpetrated by different groups of people. The Ku Klux Klan lynched over one thousand White people who were standing with Blacks by trying to get them voting rights and help.[52] It's not a person's skin color that's the problem—it is human nature, and Satan has used this. There is no reason to reject another person over the color of their skin.

In the past, Christians have been silent on the race issue. To a large degree, we have withdrawn into the four walls of our churches and our silence contributed to the situation getting out of hand. The ungodly elements in the United States of America try to pass laws that will marginalize us and take us out of the marketplace.[53] They have taken us out of education, and to a very large degree, education now is ungodly and promotes terrible things.[54] It is ruining people. It is time for us to stand up and declare the truth.

> **Did You Know?**
> Seventy percent of Christian youth renounce their faith after attending a university,[55] and approximately twenty percent of the faculty are atheists or agnostic.[56]

Society says, "You can have your light and let your light shine, but just keep it inside your four walls. You can't come out into the public square." There is an attack on Christians speaking the truth. Jesus says that we are like salt that gives flavor and preserves the earth (Matt. 5:13-16). God uses the body of Christ to preserve this earth. We have a responsibility, not only to ourselves and our immediate family but to be the salt and the light to the world. The church should have been more involved in the issue of racism. We haven't been, and now we are seeing much conflict.

The root of all the conflict in our world today, not only in our nation but in the entire world, is light against darkness. It is not White against Black or Right against Left. It is truth versus lies. It is light versus dark. People who love the dark and talk about evil, love their sin and rebellion against God. They hate people who are speaking the truth because it shows that their deeds are evil (John 3:19-20). They do not want anybody to tell them that they are wrong. Ephesians 5:13 says, *"But all things that are reproved are made manifest by the light: for whatsoever doth make manifest is light."*

God established a system of government in the church and gave it power and authority. In 1 Peter 5:2, Peter told the elders to take oversight and authority in the church. In Revelation 2–3, Jesus rebuked the pastors of those churches because they would not execute judgment on some of the people who were teaching errors in their church. Pastors make mistakes, and the way they use their power is not always from God. Our world, political system, and culture have problems because the church hasn't been salt and light the way that God called us to be.

We have a responsibility to stand up and speak out about racism. It is wrong for us to enjoy our relationship with God personally and not share these truths with other people. Not only in an evangelistic sense in which you try to reach another person, but it has been wrong for us to not be the salt and the light to our community, state, and nation. It is the truth that sets people free, and it is only the truth you know that makes you free (John 8:32). We must share the truth we know.

# CONCLUSION

Many people are consumed with hurt and hatred over the topic of racism. Politics, the media, and the education system fuel division based on skin color by distorting history. It is imperative to learn the truth of America's Black and White heroes who fought against slavery. The simple truth is there is one race—the human race.

A computer makes a good analogy to show how racism is like a software issue, not a hardware issue. Your mind is like a computer, and your body is like the computer case. It doesn't matter what color the outside of the computer case is. What matters is the apps or software it is running on. We can choose to look at what's inside people and not focus on their outer skin color.

Throughout history, racism has existed and will continue to exist until Jesus' return when sin will no longer exist. As followers of Christ, we have access to God's truth that sets us free. We can choose to see others as God sees people—without skin color or ethnicity. God's love and salvation extend to all individuals. Racism is a sin problem, and Jesus is the only answer. Our role is to share Jesus and use the Word of God as our standard to model love and unity.

# CONTINUE BUILDING YOUR BIBLICAL WORLDVIEW

**This booklet is just a brief introduction to our complete curriculum *Biblical Worldview: Racism*, which will equip you even more to respond to the issue of Racism in our world today.**

Every day, you are confronted with non-biblical worldviews coming to you through social media, the internet, and secular news sources. The Truth and Liberty Coalition (**www.truthandliberty.net**) can guide you to process current events through the lens of God's Word.

- *Live Call-in Show:* insight on current issues and callers can ask questions about biblical worldview or any topic

- *Website:* resources include a 24/7 news feed, links to other online content related to biblical worldview and current American government issues, blogs, voter guides, and prayer guides

If you enjoyed this booklet and would like more tools to arm yourself with a biblical worldview, I suggest these teachings:

- *Biblical Worldview: Racism*
- *Biblical Worldview: Foundational Truths*
- *What Is Truth?*
- *The True Nature of God*
- *Biblical Worldview* series

Some of these teachings are available for free at **awmi.net**, or they can be purchased at **awmi.net/store**.

# RECEIVE JESUS AS YOUR SAVIOR

Choosing to receive Jesus Christ as your Lord and Savior is the most important decision you'll ever make!

God's Word promises, *"That if thou shalt confess with thy mouth the Lord Jesus, and shalt believe in thine heart that God hath raised him from the dead, thou shalt be saved. For with the heart man believeth unto righteousness; and with the mouth confession is made unto salvation"* (Rom. 10:9–10). *"For whosoever shall call upon the name of the Lord shall be saved"* (Rom. 10:13). By His grace, God has already done everything to provide salvation. Your part is simply to believe and receive.

Pray out loud: "Jesus, I confess that You are my Lord and Savior. I believe in my heart that God raised You from the dead. By faith in Your Word, I receive salvation now. Thank You for saving me."

The very moment you commit your life to Jesus Christ, the truth of His Word instantly comes to pass in your spirit. Now that you're born again, there's a brand-new you!

Please contact us and let us know that you've prayed to receive Jesus as your Savior. We'd like to send you some free materials to help you on your new journey. Call our Helpline: **719-635-1111** (available 24 hours a day, seven days a week) to speak to a staff member who is here to help you understand and grow in your new relationship with the Lord.

Welcome to your new life!

# RECEIVE THE HOLY SPIRIT

As His child, your loving heavenly Father wants to give you the supernatural power you need to live a new life. *"For every one that asketh receiveth; and he that seeketh findeth; and to him that knocketh it shall be opened...how much more shall your heavenly Father give the Holy Spirit to them that ask him?"* (Luke 11:10–13).

All you have to do is ask, believe, and receive!

Pray this: "Father, I recognize my need for Your power to live a new life. Please fill me with Your Holy Spirit. By faith, I receive it right now. Thank You for baptizing me. Holy Spirit, You are welcome in my life."

Some syllables from a language you don't recognize will rise up from your heart to your mouth (1 Cor. 14:14). As you speak them out loud by faith, you're releasing God's power from within and building yourself up in the spirit (1 Cor. 14:4). You can do this whenever and wherever you like.

It doesn't really matter whether you felt anything or not when you prayed to receive the Lord and His Spirit. If you believed in your heart that you received, then God's Word promises you did. *"Therefore I say unto you, What things soever ye desire, when ye pray, believe that ye receive* **them***, and ye shall have* **them**" (Mark 11:24). God always honors His Word—believe it!

We would like to rejoice with you and help you understand more fully what has taken place in your life!

Please contact us to let us know that you've prayed to be filled with the Holy Spirit and to request the book *The New You & the Holy Spirit*. This book will explain in more detail about the benefits of being filled with the Holy Spirit and speaking in tongues. Call our Helpline: **719-635-1111** (available 24 hours a day, seven days a week).

# CALL FOR PRAYER

If you need prayer for any reason, you can call our Helpline, 24 hours a day, seven days a week at **719-635-1111**. A trained prayer minister will answer your call and pray with you.

Every day, we receive testimonies of healings and other miracles from our Helpline, and we are ministering God's nearly-too-good-to-be-true message of the Gospel to more people than ever. So, I encourage you to call today!

# ABOUT THE AUTHORS

## Abraham Hamilton III

Abraham Hamilton III has an undergraduate degree in New Testament Biblical Literature from Oral Roberts University and a juris doctor degree from Loyola University New Orleans College of Law. He is a member of the Louisiana State Bar Association, the Houston Bar Association, the Texas Bar Association, and the Federal Bar Association and is licensed to practice before all Louisiana state courts, the United States District Court for the Eastern, Middle, and Northern Districts of Louisiana, as well as all Texas state courts. Abraham currently serves the American Family Association as general counsel and public policy analyst. A father and Bible teacher, his ministerial focus includes marriage, family, apologetics, biblical worldview training, discipleship formation, and preaching. He can be found on American Family Radio's podcast *The Hamilton Corner.* Find out more about Abraham at **afr.net**.

## Alex McFarland

Alex McFarland is a Christian apologist, author, evangelist, religion and culture analyst, and advocate for biblical truth. He speaks at Christian events, conferences, debates, and other venues to teach biblical truths and preach the Gospel. He has been a spokesperson on Fox News and other media outlets. Alex is the only evangelist to have preached in all fifty states in only fifty days. His "Tour Of Truth" crusade swept across America with sixty-four evangelistic services from which came many decisions to receive Jesus and by which many Christians were equipped and encouraged. Find out more about Alex at **AlexMcFarland.com**.

## Andrew Wommack

Andrew Wommack's life was forever changed the moment he encountered the supernatural love of God on March 23, 1968. As a renowned Bible teacher and author, Andrew has made it his mission to change the way the world sees God.

Andrew's vision is to go as far and deep with the Gospel as possible. His message goes far through the *Gospel Truth* television program, which is available to over half the world's population. The message goes deep through discipleship at Charis Bible College, headquartered in Woodland Park, Colorado. Founded in 1994, Charis has campuses across the United States and around the globe. Andrew is also the president of the Truth & Liberty Coalition, an organization that seeks to educate, unify, and mobilize believers to impact culture and effect godly change on important social issues.

Andrew also has an extensive library of teaching materials in print, audio, and video. More than 200,000 hours of free teachings can be accessed at **awmi.net**.

### David Barton

David Barton is the Founder of WallBuilders, a national pro-family organization that presents America's forgotten history and heroes, with an emphasis on our moral, religious, and constitutional heritage. David is the author of numerous best-selling books and a sought-after speaker. David is also a frequent guest on several national media programs, and is a host on a daily radio show, WallBuilders Live. He serves as a consultant to state and federal legislators and has participated in several cases at the US Supreme Court. His work in media has merited several Angel Awards, Telly Awards, and the Dove Foundation Seal of Approval. Find out more about David at **WallBuilders.com.**

### E.W. Jackson

E.W. Jackson is presiding bishop of The Called Church and the founder of STAND America—Staying True to America's National Destiny. Bishop Jackson has been a guest on numerous television and radio programs, such as Fox & Friends, CBN World News, ABC's Good Morning America, and more, and he has written for the *Washington Times, American Thinker*, and other publications. He is the author of two books: *Ten Commandments to an Extraordinary Life* and the follow-up volume, *12 Principles to Make Your Life Extraordinary*. Bishop Jackson has also developed a comprehensive private-sector solution to the problems of the inner city called Project Awakening. His political career has included winning the Republican nomination for lieutenant governor of Virginia in 2013 and submitting his candidacy for the 2024 presidential election. Find out more about E.W. at **EWJackson.com**.

## Tim Barton

Tim Barton is the president of WallBuilders, a national pro-family organization that presents America's forgotten history and heroes with an emphasis on our religious, moral, and constitutional heritage. Tim excels in his various presentations on worldview, education, the truth about America's godly heritage, and a variety of other topics. From elementary students to senior adults, he captures the attention of all with his unique presentation style and powerful content. His dynamic messages speak straight to the heart while he engages and challenges the mind. An ordained minister, Tim has worked in a variety of church staff and youth mentoring positions. He speaks into the lives of those around him, encouraging them to live passionately and follow Christ wholeheartedly. Find out more about Tim at **WallBuilders.com.**

# ENDNOTES

1. Alyssa Roat, "The Samaritans: Hope from the History of a Hated People," Salem Web Network Bible Study Tools, February 23, 2023, accessed January 17, 2024, https://www.biblestudytools.com/bible-study/topical-studies/the-samaritans-hope-from-the-history-of-a-hated-people.html.

2. PBS: Public Broadcasting Service. "Africans in America: The Growing New Nation." PBS: Africans in America, accessed June 14, 2022, https://www.pbs.org/wgbh/aia/part3/map3.html.; Carter G. Woodson, PhD. "Free Negro Owners of Slaves in the United States in 1830, Together with Absentee Ownership of Slaves in the United States in 1830," Illinois University Library, University of Illinois Board of Trustees, accessed June 14, 2022, https://libsysdigi.library.illinois.edu/OCA/Books2012-02/freenegroownerso00wood/freenegroownerso00wood.pdf.

3. Rebecca Denova, "Trinity," *World History Encyclopedia*, May 3, 2021, https://www.worldhistory.org/Trinity/.

4. James O'Donnell, "St. Augustine," *Encyclopedia Britannica*, May 11, 2022, https://www.britannica.com/biography/Saint-Augustine.

5. Henry Chadwick, trans., *Confessions*, (Oxford's World Classics), Oxford: Oxford University Press, 2008.

6. "Martin Luther and Ethiopian Christianity: Historical Traces," The University of Chicago Divinity School, November 2, 2017, https://divinity.uchicago.edu/sightings/articles/martin-luther-and-ethiopian-christianity-historical-traces.

7. *Blue Letter Bible*, s.v. "G1484-ethnos–Strong's Greek Lexicon (NKJV)," accessed January 19, 2042, https://www.blueletterbible.org/lexicon/g1484/nkjv/tr/0-1/.

8. Elizabeth Kolbert, "There's No Scientific Basis for Race—It's a Made-up Label," *National Geographic*, Simon & Schuster, Inc., October 22, 2018, https://www.nationalgeographic.co.uk/people-and-culture/2018/04/theres-no-scientific-basis-for-race-its-a-made-up-label.

9. Suzanne Rowan Kelleher "How a Museum's Human Skull Collection Sparked a Racial Reckoning," *Forbes Magazine*, April 18, 2021, https://www.forbes.com/sites/suzannerowankelleher/2021/04/16/penn-museum-samuel-morton-human-skull-collection-black-slaves-repatriation/?sh=d893e457d4c9; "1770s–1850s: One Race or Several Species?" *NBC News*, NBC Universal News Group, May 27, 2008, https://www.nbcnews.com/id/wbna24714532.

10. *Blue Letter Bible*, s.v. "G2842-koinōnia–Strong's Greek Lexicon (NKJV)," accessed July 31, 2022. https://www.blueletterbible.org/lexicon/g2842/nkjv/tr/0-1/.

11. Michael L. Lanning, "The Assessment: Numbers, Influence, Results," in *African Americans in the Revolutionary War*, New York, NY: Kensington Publishing Corporation, 2021.

12. Michael L. Lanning, "Segregated Freedom Fighters: All Black Units," in *African Americans in the Revolutionary War*.

13. "Peter Salem and the Battle of Bunker Hill," National Museum of African American History and Culture, Smithsonian, March 15, 2017, https:// nmaahc.si.edu/explore/stories/peter-salem-and-battle-bunker-hill.

14. "Peter Salem," American Battlefield Trust, accessed August 3, 2022, https://www.battlefields.org/learn/biographies/peter-salem.

15. Thaddeus Morgan, "How an Enslaved Man-Turned-Spy Helped Secure Victory at the Battle of Yorktown," *History.com*, A&E Television Networks, August 21, 2023, https://www.history.com/news/battle-of-yorktown-slave-spy-james-armistead .

16. "Americans Defeat the British at Yorktown," *History.com*, A&E Television Networks, October 16, 2020, https://www.history.com/this-day-in-history/victory-at-yorktown.

17. Don Jordan and Michael Walsh, *White Cargo: The Forgotten History of Britain's White Slaves in America*, New York, NY: New York University Press, 2008.

18. Michael F. Doran "Negro Slaves of the Five Civilized Tribes," *Annals of the Association of American Geographers* 68, no. 3 (1978): 335–50, http://www.jstor.org/stable/2561972.

19. J. Gordon Hylton, "When Did Slavery Really End in the United States?" *Marquette University Law School Faculty Blog*, Marquette University Law School, January 15, 2013, https://law.marquette.edu/

facultyblog/2013/01/when-did-slavery-really-end-in-the-united-states/comment-page-1/.

20. Amy Tikkan, "I Have a Dream," *Encyclopedia Britannica*, January 13, 2024, https://www.britannica.com/topic/I-Have-A-Dream.

21. "The Declaration of Independence," *Archives.gov*, U.S. National Archives and Records Administration, accessed January 17, 2024, https://www.archives.gov/founding-docs/declaration.

22. "African Participation and Resistance to the Trade," *African Passages, Lowcountry Adaptations*, Lowcountry Digital History Initiative, accessed July 3, 2022, https://ldhi.library.cofc.edu/exhibits/show/africanpassageslowcountryadapt/introductionatlanticworld/african_participation_and_resi.; David Smith, "African Chiefs Urged to Apologise for Slave Trade," *The Guardian. Guardian News and Media*, November 18, 2009, https://www.theguardian.com/world/2009/nov/18/africans-apologise-slave-trade.; Stephen McDowell, "The Bible, Slavery, and America's Founders," WallBuilders, May 2912, 20213, https://wallbuilders.com/resource/the-bible-slavery-and-americas-founders/.; "The Origins of American Slavery," AP Central, College Board, accessed August 16, 2022, https://apcentral.collegeboard.org/series/america-on-the-world-stage/origins-american-slavery.

23. "This Deplorable Entanglement," *Monticello.org*, Monticello and the University of Virginia, accessed August 7, 2022, https://www.monticello.org/slavery/paradox-of-liberty/thomas-jefferson-liberty-slavery/this-deplorable-entanglement/; Gordon Lloyd and Jenny S. Martinez, "The Slave Trade Clause: Common

Interpretation," National Constitution Center, accessed August 7, 2022, https://constitutioncenter.org/the-constitution/articles/article-i/clauses/761#the-slave-trade-clause-lloyd-martinez.

24. Frank Freidel and Hugh Sidey, "Abraham Lincoln," *Whitehouse.gov*, The White House, The United States Government, January 15, 2021, https://www.whitehouse.gov/about-the-white-house/presidents/abraham- lincoln/; J.L. Weber and Warren W. Hassler, "American Civil War," *Encyclopedia Britannica*, July 30, 2022, https://www.britannica.com/event/American-Civil-War.

25. "The Civil Rights Bill of 1866," US House of Representatives: History, Art & Archives, accessed January 17, 2024, https://history.house.gov/Historical-Highlights/1851-1900/The-Civil-Rights-Bill-of-1866/.

26. Melvin I. Urofsky, "Jim Crow Law," *Encyclopedia Britannica*, December 29, 2023, https://www.britannica.com/event/Jim-Crow-law.;"A Brief History of Civil Rights in the United States: Jim Crow Era," Howard University School of Law Library, Howard University, accessed August 11, 2022. https://library.law. howard.edu/civilrightshistory/blackrights/jimcrow.

27. "Judeo-Christian Roots of America's Founding Ideals and Documents,"  National Center for Constitutional Studies, accessed January 17, 2024,  https://nccs.net/blogs/articles/judeo-christian-roots-of-americas-founding-ideals-and-documents; "Jefferson's Attitudes toward Slavery," *Monticello.org*, Monticello and the University of Virginia, accessed August 7, 2022, https://www. monticello.org/thomas-jefferson/

jefferson-slavery/jefferson-s- attitudes-toward-slavery/.

28. Bobbie T. Teague, "Education," in *Cane Creek, Mother of Meetings*, 106–112, Snow Camp, NC: Cane Creek Monthly Meeting of Friends, 1995, accessed January 17, 2024, https://archive.org/details/canecreekmothero01teag/page/106/mode/2up.

29. Betty D. Renfer, "Learning in Colonial Carolina," *NCpedia.org*, Anchor: A North Carolina History Online Resource, accessed August 7, 2022, https://www.ncpedia.org/anchor/learning-colonial-carolina.

30. Thomas W. Hagedorn, *Founding Zealots: How Evangelicals Created America's First Public Schools, 1783–1865*, Cincinnati, OH: Christian History in America LLC, 2013.

31. Roger Schultz, "Christianity and the American University," *Liberty Journal*, Liberty University, February 26, 2019, https://www.liberty.edu/journal/article/christianity-and-the-american-university/.

32. John R. McKivigan, *The War Against Proslavery Religion: Abolitionism and the Northern Churches, 1830–1865*, Cornell University Press, 1984, http://www.jstor.org/stable/10.7591/j.ctv2n7mq7.

33. Brian Flood and David Rutz, "UnAmerican Express: Critics Launch Campaign Against 'Racially Divisive Policies' at Credit Card Giant," Fox News, FOX News Network, March 23, 2022, https://www.foxnews.com/media/unamerican-express-critics-launch-campaign-against- racially-divisive-policies-at-credit-card-giant.

34. Karl Marx and Friedrich Engels, "The Communist Manifesto: Marx, Karl, 1818–1883," Internet Archive, New York, Monthly Review Press, January 1, 1964, https://archive.org/details/communistmani00marx/page/n5/mode/2up?q=class%2Brevolution.

35. Manning Johnson, *Color, Communism, and Common Sense: A True Story*. Eureka, MT: Lighthouse Trails, 2021; "Founder of Italian Communist Party Converted before Death," Catholic News Agency. Catholic News Agency, December 2, 2008, https://www.catholicnewsagency.com/news/14501/founder-of-italian-communist-party-converted-before-death.

36. Mike Gonzalez, "Marxism Underpins Black Lives Matter Agenda," The Heritage Foundation, September 8, 2021, https://www.heritage.org/progressivism/commentary/marxism-underpins-black-lives-matter-agenda.

37. Heather Mac Donald, "The First Black Lives Matter Wave Led to 2K Extra Black Homicides – but New Wave Will Be Worse," *New York Post*, NYP Holdings, Inc., July 3, 2020, https://nypost.com/2020/07/03/new-black-lives-matter-wave-will-lead-to-more-black-homicides-than-first/; "Crime in the U.S. 2019," FBI – Expanded Homicide Data Table 6, Federal Bureau of Investigation, accessed December 17, 2024, https://ucr.fbi.gov/crime-in-the-u.s/2019/crime-in-the-u.s.-2019/tables/expanded-homicide-data-table-6.xls.

38. "Fulton Sheen: Communism and Truth," WQPH Radio 89.3 FM, WQPH, September 24, 2020, https://wqphradio.org/2020/09/fulton-sheen-communism-and-truth/.

39. "Declaration of Independence," *Archives.org*, U.S. National Archives and Records Administration, accessed January 17, 2024, https://www.archives.gov/founding-docs/declaration.

40. *Merriam-Webster Dictionary*, s.v. "Identity Politics Definition & Meaning," accessed August 24, 2022, https://www.merriam- webster.com/dictionary/identity%20politics.

41. Christine Douglass-Williams "Identity Politics, Oppression and Aversion to the White Man," *Front Page Magazine*, David Horowitz Freedom Center, July 15, 2020, https://www.frontpagemag.com/identity-politics-oppression-and-aversion-white-christine-douglass-williams/.

42. Heath W. Carter, "Woodrow Wilson's Troubling Faith," *The Christian Century*, June 26, 2017, https://www.christiancentury.org/review/books/woodrow-wilson-s-troubling-faith.

43. "Woodrow Wilson." The White House, The United States Government, January 15, 2021, https://www.whitehouse.gov/about-the-white- house/presidents/woodrow-wilson/.

44. Woodrow Wilson, *A History of the American People*, Vol. 2, New York, NY: Harper and Brothers, 1901.

45. Theodore Roosevelt, "Americanism," *The Project Gutenberg eBook of Americanism, by Theodore Roosevelt*, Project Gutenberg, May 22, 2022, https://www.gutenberg.org/files/68152/68152-h/68152-h.htm.

46. W.E.B. Du Bois, "The Trading Colonies," in *The Suppression of the African Slave-Trade to the*

*United States of America 1638-1870*, New York, NY: Longmans, Green, and Co., 1896; Jillian Galle, "Servants and Masters in the Plymouth Colony," The Plymouth Colony Archive Project, December 14, 2007, http://www.histarch.illinois.edu/plymouth/galle1.html.

47. Conor Friedersdorf, "1776 Honors America's Diversity in a Way 1619 Does Not," *The Atlantic*, Atlantic Media Company, January 6, 2020, https://www.theatlantic.com/ideas/archive/2020/01/inclusive-case-1776-not-1619/604435/; "New York Times Quietly Edits '1619 Project' after Conservative Pushback," The Heritage Foundation, September 26, 2020, https://www.heritage.org/american-founders/impact/new-york-times-quietly-edits-1619-project-after-conservative-pushback.

48. Maria Baghramian and J. Adam Carter, "Relativism," *Stanford Encyclopedia of Philosophy*, The Metaphysics Research Lab, Department of Philosophy, Stanford University, September 15, 2020, https://plato.stanford.edu/entries/relativism/.

49. Sam Waldron, "Law of Non-Contradiction," Christian Apologetics & Research Ministry, accessed September 16, 2022. https://carm.org/dictionary/law-of-non-contradiction/; Paula Gottlieb, "Aristotle on Non-Contradiction," *Stanford Encyclopedia of Philosophy*, The Metaphysics Research Lab, Department of Philosophy, Stanford University, March 6, 2019, https:// plato.stanford.edu/entries/aristotle-noncontradiction/.

50. Anthony J.P. Kenny and Alselm H. Amadio , "Aristotle," *Encyclopedia Britannica*, January 5, 2024, https://www.britannica.com/biography/Aristotle.

51. *Online Etymology Dictionary*, s.v. "Egalitarianism (n.)," Douglas Harper, accessed October 26, 2022, https://www.etymonline.com/word/egalitarianism#etymonline_v_32186.

52. Richard Emanuel, "Many Whites Were Lynched for Fighting Racism," *Montgomery Advertiser*, September 25, 2017. https://www.montgomeryadvertiser.com/story/opinion/2017/09/25/ many-whites-were-lynched-fighting-racism-opinion/700690001/; "Lynchings: By State and Race, 1882-1968," *Tuskegee University Archives Repository*, Tuskegee University, accessed November 7, 2022, http://archive.tuskegee.edu/repository/wp-content/uploads/2020/11/Lynchings-Stats-Year-Dates-Causes.pdf.

53. "Religious Freedom: What's at Stake If We Lose It," *Heritage Explains*, The Heritage Foundation, accessed November 7, 2022, https://www.heritage.org/religious-liberty/heritage-explains/religious-freedom-whats-stake-if-we-lose-it.

54. John R. Vile, "Pfeiffer v. Board of Education," *The First Amendment Encyclopedia*, Middle Tennessee State University, December 15, 2023, https://firstamendment.mtsu.edu/article/pfeiffer-v-board-of-education/.

55. Nick Petrusha, "College Students Losing Their Faith," *Helena Independent Record*, January 29, 2022, https://helenair.com/news/local/nick-petrusha-column-college-students-losing-their-faith/article94a95ee7-8271-54ce-a239-0ff416c223eb.html.

56. Neil Gross and Solon Simmons, "How Religious Are America's College and University Professors?" Social

Science Research Council, February 6, 2007, http://religion.ssrc.org/reforum/Gross_Simmons.pdf.

# CONTACT INFORMATION

**Andrew Wommack Ministries, Inc.**
PO Box 3333
Colorado Springs, CO 80934-3333
info@awmi.net
**awmi.net**

Helpline: 719-635-1111 (available 24/7)

**Charis Bible College**
info@charisbiblecollege.org
844-360-9577
**CharisBibleCollege.org**

For a complete list of our offices, visit **awmi.net/contact-us.**

Connect with us on social media.